Young Learner's
LOOK-n-LEARN ANIMALS

© Young Learner Publications®, India

Alligator

An alligator has sharp teeth that help it to eat small animals in a single bite. It has a wide and U-shaped snout.

Anteater

An anteater has no teeth. It uses its long and sticky tongue to catch ants and termites. It sleeps for 15 hours per day.

Armadillo

An armadillo has an armour-like leathery shell on its back. It eats ants and grubs. It loves digging. It has poor eyesight.

Bandicoot

A bandicoot is found in Australia. It eats both plants and animals. It carries its young one in its pouch.

Bat

A bat is the only flying mammal. It is active at night and can live for over 20 years. It feeds on insects, fish and fruits.

Bear

A bear is a wild animal. It likes to eat honey. It sleeps for days at a stretch during winters.

Beaver

A beaver can live in water as well as on land. It belongs to the rodent family. It is known to build dams.

Bobcat

A bobcat is a huge cat with a short tail. It is a wild animal. It is a great hunter and can leap up to 10 feet to get to its prey.

Buffalo

A buffalo is a domestic animal that looks similar to a cow. It is reared for its milk. It makes a mooing sound.

Camel

A camel is also called the ship of the desert. It can drink up to 40 gallons of water at a time. It stores fat in its hump.

Cat

A cat is a pet animal. It makes a mewing sound. It has sharp hearing. Its baby is called a kitten.

Cheetah

The cheetah is the fastest land animal. It can reach a top speed of around 113 km/h. It belongs to the cat family.

Chimpanzee

A chimpanzee is a member of the ape family. Its arms are longer than its legs. It can make tools to help it get food.

Chinchilla

A chinchilla is a rodent. It is slightly larger than a squirrel. It is most active during dawn and dusk.

Cow

A cow is a domestic animal. It gives us milk and meat. It lives in a shed and makes a mooing sound.

Crocodile

A crocodile is a large reptile. It is a good swimmer. It is found in fresh water bodies. It has a V-shaped snout.

Deer

A deer likes to eat grass. It is a light-footed, shy animal. It is often hunted by large carnivorous animals.

Dog

A dog is a very loyal pet animal. It is known as man's best friend. It has a remarkable sense of smell.

Dolphin

A dolphin is a mammal that lives in the sea. It mostly eats fish and squid. A group of dolphins is called a school.

Donkey

A donkey is a domestic animal. It makes a braying sound. It is used to carry loads, so it is also called the beast of burden.

Elephant

The elephant is the largest land animal. It has a long trunk and big ears. It makes a trumpeting sound.

Fish

A fish is a water animal. It has gills that help it breathe, and fins that help it swim. It can eat plants and animals.

Fox

A fox has triangular ears and a long bushy tail. It is often said to be a clever animal. It is a great night-time hunter.

Frog

A frog lives on land and in water. It makes a croaking sound. A baby frog is called a tadpole.

Giant panda

The giant panda belongs to the bear family. It has black patches around its eyes. It mostly eats bamboo, though sometimes it also eats rodents and birds.

Giraffe

A giraffe is a wild animal. It has a long neck and small horns on its head. Its long neck enables it to eat leaves from tall trees.

Goat

A goat can climb mountains easily. It makes a bleating sound. It is reared for its milk and meat.

Gorilla

A gorilla can communicate using sign language. It mostly eats plants and uses its knuckles to walk.

Hamster

A hamster is a rodent. It eats seeds, fruits and vegetation. It is often kept as a pet. It is an excellent digger and uses its senses of smell and touch to navigate.

Hippopotamus

A hippopotamus is a huge mammal with a large mouth and teeth, and a hairless body. It spends its time in water and mud.

Horse

A horse runs very fast. It makes a neighing sound. The young one of a horse is called a foal.

Hyena

A hyena is a wild animal. It grabs its prey by its teeth. It is good at running and making sharp turns.

Iguana

An iguana is a huge lizard that eats plants. It has a very good eyesight. It is often kept as a pet.

Jackal

A jackal has long legs and curved teeth. It is most active at dawn and dusk. It hunts small mammals, birds and reptiles.

Kangaroo

A kangaroo is found in Australia. The female kangaroo has a pouch on its belly to carry its baby.

Koala

A koala is found in Australia. It has round, fluffy ears. It likes to eat eucalyptus leaves. It lives up to 20 years in the wild.

Lemur

A lemur is found in Madagascar. It eats fruits, leaves and insects. It has a long snout. It is the smallest primate.

Leopard

A leopard has a long body and short legs. Its body is covered with spots. It is a member of the cat family.

Lion

A lion is also called the king of the jungle. It has a thick mane and makes a roaring sound. It hunts and eats other animals.

Lizard

A lizard is seen crawling on walls. It eats flies and other insects by catching them with its tongue.

Lynx

A lynx is a wild cat. It has a short tail and tufts of black hair on its ears. It can climb trees and swim fast.

Meerkat

A meerkat belongs to the mongoose family. It lives in groups with its clan. It is mostly found in Africa.

Mongoose

A mongoose is a wild animal. It eats insects, crabs, lizards, snakes and rodents. It is good at fighting snakes.

Monkey

A monkey lives on trees and in grasslands. It mostly eats plants, fruits, leaves, seeds, nuts and small animals.

Mouse

A mouse is a small mammal. It has small, rounded ears and no hair on its long tail. It makes a squeaking sound.

Orangutan

An orangutan has reddish-brown hair and grey-black skin. It is also called red ape. It mostly lives on trees and eats fruits.

Otter

An otter lives in water and on land. It has webbed paws. It eats fish, frogs, crabs, small mammals and birds.

Panther

A panther looks black in colour, but its fur is a mix of blue, black, grey and purple colours. It has silver-grey eyes.

Puma

A puma has the largest hind legs in the cat family. It is the second heaviest cat in the world. It can't roar like a lion or jaguar.

Rhinoceros

A rhinoceros has one or two horns on its nose. Its skin is very thick, more than 1.5 cm, which works like an armour. It has sharp senses of smell and hearing.

Snake

A snake is a long, scaly reptile. It may or may not be poisonous. It can shed its entire skin and grow a new one.

Squirrel

A squirrel has a bushy tail. It can climb trees and is very quick. It loves eating nuts and seeds.

Tiger

The tiger is the largest member of the cat family. It spends a lot of its time in lakes, rivers, etc. It can kill animals over twice its size.

Toad

A toad has a dry, bumpy skin and short legs. A group of toads is called a knot. It can live up to 35 years in captivity. Venom of cane toads is lethal.

Tortoise

A tortoise is a reptile. It lives on land. It has a hard shell on its back. It lays eggs. It mostly eats plants.

Turtle

A turtle lives in the sea and fresh water bodies. Though it lives in water, it lays its eggs on land.

Walrus

A walrus is a large mammal with long tusks and whiskers. It has large flippers that help it swim.

Whale

The whale is the largest mammal in the world. It breathes through the blowhole on its back.

Wolf

A wolf has excellent hearing, eyesight and a keen sense of smell. It is the largest member of the dog family.

Zebra

A zebra is a wild animal. It has black and white stripes on its body. Each zebra has a unique pattern of stripes.